HAL•LEONARD
INSTRUMENTAL
PLAY-ALONG

AUDIO
ACCESS
INCLUDED

PLAYBACK+
Speed • Pitch • Balance • Loop

HORN

CHRISTMAS Favorites

Audio arrangements by Peter Deneff

To access audio visit:
www.halleonard.com/mylibrary
Enter Code
7446-7084-0493-0329

ISBN 978-1-4950-9638-9

7777 W. BLUEMOUND RD. P.O. BOX 13819 MILWAUKEE, WI 53213

In Australia Contact:
Hal Leonard Australia Pty. Ltd.
4 Lentara Court
Cheltenham, Victoria, 3192 Australia
Email: ausadmin@halleonard.com.au

Visit Hal Leonard Online at
www.halleonard.com

BLUE CHRISTMAS

Horn

Words and Music by BILLY HAYES
and JAY JOHNSON

THE CHRISTMAS SONG
(Chestnuts Roasting on an Open Fire)

Horn

Music and Lyric by MEL TORMÉ
and ROBERT WELLS

CHRISTMAS TIME IS HERE

from A CHARLIE BROWN CHRISTMAS

Horn

Words by LEE MENDELSON
Music by VINCE GUARALDI

FELIZ NAVIDAD

Horn

Music and Lyrics by
JOSÉ FELICIANO

HAPPY XMAS
(War Is Over)

Horn

Written by JOHN LENNON
and YOKO ONO

HAVE YOURSELF A MERRY LITTLE CHRISTMAS
from MEET ME IN ST. LOUIS

Horn

Words and Music by HUGH MARTIN
and RALPH BLANE

HERE COMES SANTA CLAUS
(Right Down Santa Claus Lane)

HORN

Words and Music by GENE AUTRY
and OAKLEY HALDEMAN

(There's No Place Like)
HOME FOR THE HOLIDAYS

HORN

Words and Music by AL STILLMAN
and ROBERT ALLEN

Moderately

Electric Piano

IT'S BEGINNING TO LOOK LIKE CHRISTMAS

Horn

By MEREDITH WILLSON

MELE KALIKIMAKA

Horn

Words and Music by
R. ALEX ANDERSON

MERRY CHRISTMAS, DARLING

Horn

Words and Music by RICHARD CARPENTER
and FRANK POOLER

ROCKIN' AROUND THE CHRISTMAS TREE

Horn

Music and Lyrics by
JOHNNY MARKS

RUDOLPH THE RED-NOSED REINDEER

HORN

Music and Lyrics by
JOHNNY MARKS

SILVER AND GOLD

HORN

Music and Lyrics by
JOHNNY MARKS

HAL•LEONARD INSTRUMENTAL PLAY-ALONG

Your favorite songs are arranged just for solo instrumentalists with this outstanding series. Each book includes a great full-accompaniment play-along audio so you can sound just like a pro! Check out www.halleonard.com to see all the titles available.

The Beatles

All You Need Is Love • Blackbird • Day Tripper • Eleanor Rigby • Get Back • Here, There and Everywhere • Hey Jude • I Will • Let It Be • Lucy in the Sky with Diamonds • Ob-La-Di, Ob-La-Da • Penny Lane • Something • Ticket to Ride • Yesterday.

	00225330	Flute	$14.99
	00225331	Clarinet	$14.99
	00225332	Alto Sax	$14.99
	00225333	Tenor Sax	$14.99
	00225334	Trumpet	$14.99
	00225335	Horn	$14.99
	00225336	Trombone	$14.99
	00225337	Violin	$14.99
	00225338	Viola	$14.99
	00225339	Cello	$14.99

Chart Hits

All About That Bass • All of Me • Happy • Radioactive • Roar • Say Something • Shake It Off • A Sky Full of Stars • Someone like You • Stay with Me • Thinking Out Loud • Uptown Funk.

	00146207	Flute	$12.99
	00146208	Clarinet	$12.99
	00146209	Alto Sax	$12.99
	00146210	Tenor Sax	$12.99
	00146211	Trumpet	$12.99
	00146212	Horn	$12.99
	00146213	Trombone	$12.99
	00146214	Violin	$12.99
	00146215	Viola	$12.99
	00146216	Cello	$12.99

Coldplay

Clocks • Every Teardrop Is a Waterfall • Fix You • In My Place • Lost! • Paradise • The Scientist • Speed of Sound • Trouble • Violet Hill • Viva La Vida • Yellow.

	00103337	Flute	$12.99
	00103338	Clarinet	$12.99
	00103339	Alto Sax	$12.99
	00103340	Tenor Sax	$12.99
	00103341	Trumpet	$12.99
	00103342	Horn	$12.99
	00103343	Trombone	$12.99
	00103344	Violin	$12.99
	00103345	Viola	$12.99
	00103346	Cello	$12.99

Disney Greats

Arabian Nights • Hawaiian Roller Coaster Ride • It's a Small World • Look Through My Eyes • Yo Ho (A Pirate's Life for Me) • and more.

	00841934	Flute	$12.99
	00841935	Clarinet	$12.99
	00841936	Alto Sax	$12.99
	00841937	Tenor Sax	$12.95
	00841938	Trumpet	$12.99
	00841939	Horn	$12.99
	00841940	Trombone	$12.95
	00841941	Violin	$12.99
	00841942	Viola	$12.99
	00841943	Cello	$12.99
	00842078	Oboe	$12.99

Great Themes

Bella's Lullaby • Chariots of Fire • Get Smart • Hawaii Five-O Theme • I Love Lucy • The Odd Couple • Spanish Flea • and more.

	00842468	Flute	$12.99
	00842469	Clarinet	$12.99
	00842470	Alto Sax	$12.99
	00842471	Tenor Sax	$12.99
	00842472	Trumpet	$12.99
	00842473	Horn	$12.99
	00842474	Trombone	$12.99
	00842475	Violin	$12.99
	00842476	Viola	$12.99
	00842477	Cello	$12.99

Popular Hits

Breakeven • Fireflies • Halo • Hey, Soul Sister • I Gotta Feeling • I'm Yours • Need You Now • Poker Face • Viva La Vida • You Belong with Me • and more.

	00842511	Flute	$12.99
	00842512	Clarinet	$12.99
	00842513	Alto Sax	$12.99
	00842514	Tenor Sax	$12.99
	00842515	Trumpet	$12.99
	00842516	Horn	$12.99
	00842517	Trombone	$12.99
	00842518	Violin	$12.99
	00842519	Viola	$12.99
	00842520	Cello	$12.99

Songs from Frozen, Tangled and Enchanted

Do You Want to Build a Snowman? • For the First Time in Forever • Happy Working Song • I See the Light • In Summer • Let It Go • Mother Knows Best • That's How You Know • True Love's First Kiss • When Will My Life Begin • and more.

	00126921	Flute	$14.99
	00126922	Clarinet	$14.99
	00126923	Alto Sax	$14.99
	00126924	Tenor Sax	$14.99
	00126925	Trumpet	$14.99
	00126926	Horn	$14.99
	00126927	Trombone	$14.99
	00126928	Violin	$14.99
	00126929	Viola	$14.99
	00126930	Cello	$14.99

Top Hits

Adventure of a Lifetime • Budapest • Die a Happy Man • Ex's & Oh's • Fight Song • Hello • Let It Go • Love Yourself • One Call Away • Pillowtalk • Stitches • Writing's on the Wall.

	00171073	Flute	$12.99
	00171074	Clarinet	$12.99
	00171075	Alto Sax	$12.99
	00171106	Tenor Sax	$12.99
	00171107	Trumpet	$12.99
	00171108	Horn	$12.99
	00171109	Trombone	$12.99
	00171110	Violin	$12.99
	00171111	Viola	$12.99
	00171112	Cello	$12.99

Wicked

As Long As You're Mine • Dancing Through Life • Defying Gravity • For Good • I'm Not That Girl • Popular • The Wizard and I • and more.

	00842236	Flute	$12.99
	00842237	Clarinet	$12.99
	00842238	Alto Saxophone	$11.95
	00842239	Tenor Saxophone	$11.95
	00842240	Trumpet	$11.99
	00842241	Horn	$11.95
	00842242	Trombone	$12.99
	00842243	Violin	$11.99
	00842244	Viola	$12.99
	00842245	Cello	$12.99

HAL•LEONARD®